Ibadah

When love transforms into transcendence,
life transforms into servitude.

by

Ankur Kalra, MD

The contents of this work, including, but not limited to, the accuracy of events, people, and places depicted; opinions expressed; permission to use previously published materials included; and any advice given or actions advocated are solely the responsibility of the author, who assumes all liability for said work and indemnifies the publisher against any claims stemming from publication of the work.

All Rights Reserved
Copyright © 2020 by Ankur Kalra, MD

No part of this book may be reproduced or transmitted, downloaded, distributed, reverse engineered, or stored in or introduced into any information storage and retrieval system, in any form or by any means, including photocopying and recording, whether electronic or mechanical, now known or hereinafter invented without permission in writing from the publisher.

Dorrance Publishing Co
585 Alpha Drive
Suite 103
Pittsburgh, PA 15238
Visit our website at *www.dorrancebookstore.com*

ISBN: 978-1-6453-0804-1
eISBN: 978-1-6461-0553-3

A prelude to a love story from 286 B.C.
that will change your perception of love, forever.

The Healing Power of Poetry

Language is the thread that weaves together our collective stories made of the colors of pain, suffering, joy, and longing. What are we without language? Even our thoughts and memories are but fragments of words and sounds. As poignant as prose is, poetry is the crowning glory of language.

Poetry borders on the mystical, where words string themselves together as the essence of a lived experience. A poet's words touch the reader such that the essence of the experience is absorbed and even if it isn't *their* lived experience, it is felt as if it is. In that instance, the thread of language has irrevocably bound the poet and the reader in an invisible, intimate bond. Poetry is revered because this is the kind of deep connection that each of us longs for.

In this collection, Ankur Kalra binds us all through his deeply moving words. Love, loss, sweetness, mystery, angst—these are lived experiences for each of us. And in reading his words, we are bound together in the sacredness of humanity. Ankur isn't just a wonderful poet. He's a well-known interventional cardiologist who brings his vulnerability and compassion to his day-to-day grind. He knows a thing or two about the organ that pumps blood! Yet, the heart he allows us to access here is the subtler one—the one that drives us all to be who we are. And this is precisely what makes this collection so unique. Like Ankur, it heals.

May this collection of poems find its mark in the hearts of all its readers, and bring us together in the love and understanding of our shared dreams and hopes. This is the kind of healing this world so desperately needs.

Kavitha Chinnaiyan, M.D.
Northville, MI

The feeling of heartbreak is something that feels so wholly human. It drops us into the full spectrum of our emotional experience and offers a pathway of connection we can all relate to through shared experience.

The opportunity to translate Dr. Kalra's poetry into a visual experience was immediately inspiring for me, even more so once I learned he wanted the artwork to express the lesson learned through each step of heartbreak.

Each piece was painted using handmade earth pigment watercolor paints in my Ojai, California studio.

I began the process by reducing each poem to the core emotion/theme I felt while reading. I then reflected on what I've personally learned from those emotions in my own separation. After finding the lesson in each piece, I meditated on what that lesson felt like in my body and converted that sensation into a minimal, abstract painting.

I wanted to maintain the rawness felt during heartbreak so I allowed the lines of each piece to be organic and imperfect. The use of earth pigments also served as a reminder that even when separation feels chaotic, there is always stability within and below us.

- Vyana Novus

LESSON:
Be in the present moment, cultivate patience, heal the past.

Sacrifice or Mistake

"My soul is restless, it is combust but the pain just does not dissipate,
Rejection was a bolt from the blue and chilling,
why didn't our souls conflate?
My world has collapsed, my spirit is oblate,
I still can't fathom how it was so easy
for them to separate, for me, life is a checkmate.
"Because we're attracted to one another,"
if it was just attraction for them, I must've exercised
caution and not let emotions govern my mandate.
The decision to come together was consensual,
their solitary resolve to walk away overnight was my fate,
Perhaps they deserved better, but it was unfair
to not share if they ever felt anything legitimate.
My heart and love are as honest as His presence,
still He let their essence abrogate,
I had a prescription for pain in my destiny,
I requested Him to give me their share as well, in lieu of
letting me know if their decision was realization
of a sacrifice or a mistake delicate."

LESSON:
Trust yourself, surrender to the river of life, trust the flow of life and move with its natural rhythms.

Foreigner

"'It feels right,' I naively believed in every word that was said.
I thought we were soulmates, I was thinking of getting wed.
Perhaps I heard what they never said,
my emotions and intentions were on a different sled.
It was such an emotional connection for me (was it)
for them just a physical tête-à-tête?
I'm a foreigner in a new land, perhaps I should have learned
the ropes and the rules, before executing my exotic mindset."

LESSON:
How to set boundaries and fully see the self as independent from another.

Transient Attraction

"I praised you through baring my soul, it was panegyrical.
I didn't have to look elsewhere but in your eyes, my love was that real.
I held you in my arms, my passion was veritable.
I kissed you slow, it was most magical and surreal.
Discerning that your exotic attraction was transient was devastating, my love, however, was spiritual."

LESSON:
How to uphold boundaries, not as a confining or restricting presence, but as a liberating action.

Paralyzed

"I crave for your presence, without you my existence has pulverized,
I yearn to look into your eyes, without words, they have me eulogized.
Why did He cultivate this love for you in my heart,
if this boat was destined to be capsized?
I don't know what I did to have this destiny,
no heart with love deserves to be penalized,
Without you in my life, my soul feels vandalized.
The mere thought of you with someone else, makes me paralyzed."

LESSON:
Acceptance of life moving differently than desired.

Kiss

"It was cold and dark, your eyes were the only source of glow,
I vividly remember every breath and pulse, time had ceased to flow.
Living in the moment is the way to live,
I'll literally do anything for Him for it to bestow,
My heart stops each time I reminisce the moment
I kissed you the first time, slow.
The heavens approved it as well, He blessed us with snow."

LESSON:
Acceptance and understanding of another's perspective and experiences.

Love

"To care for you is love,
To celebrate you is love,
To remember little things about you is love,
To reminisce moments with you is love,
To miss you is love,
To cherish you is love,
To be unconditional is love,
To still love despite differences is love,
To return animosity with love is love,
To forgive is love,
To pray for you is love,
To create your legacy is love,
To love you is love,
I know you can't relate to it,
Perhaps I came into your life to teach you what's love."

LESSON:
Stand on your feet with the funnel of truth flowing from source to self.

Relentless

"I achieved milestones, I conquered frontiers,
I fought battles, I dismantled barriers.
The warrior in me was always austere,
You ignited this relentless flame in my heart,
It just doesn't disappear.
I've always stood chin up, ain't matter if they're kings or brigadiers,
There's a colossal reason why I always bow down to you,
There is no ego, even self-respect shears.
'Tis the admiration and love that only He shares."

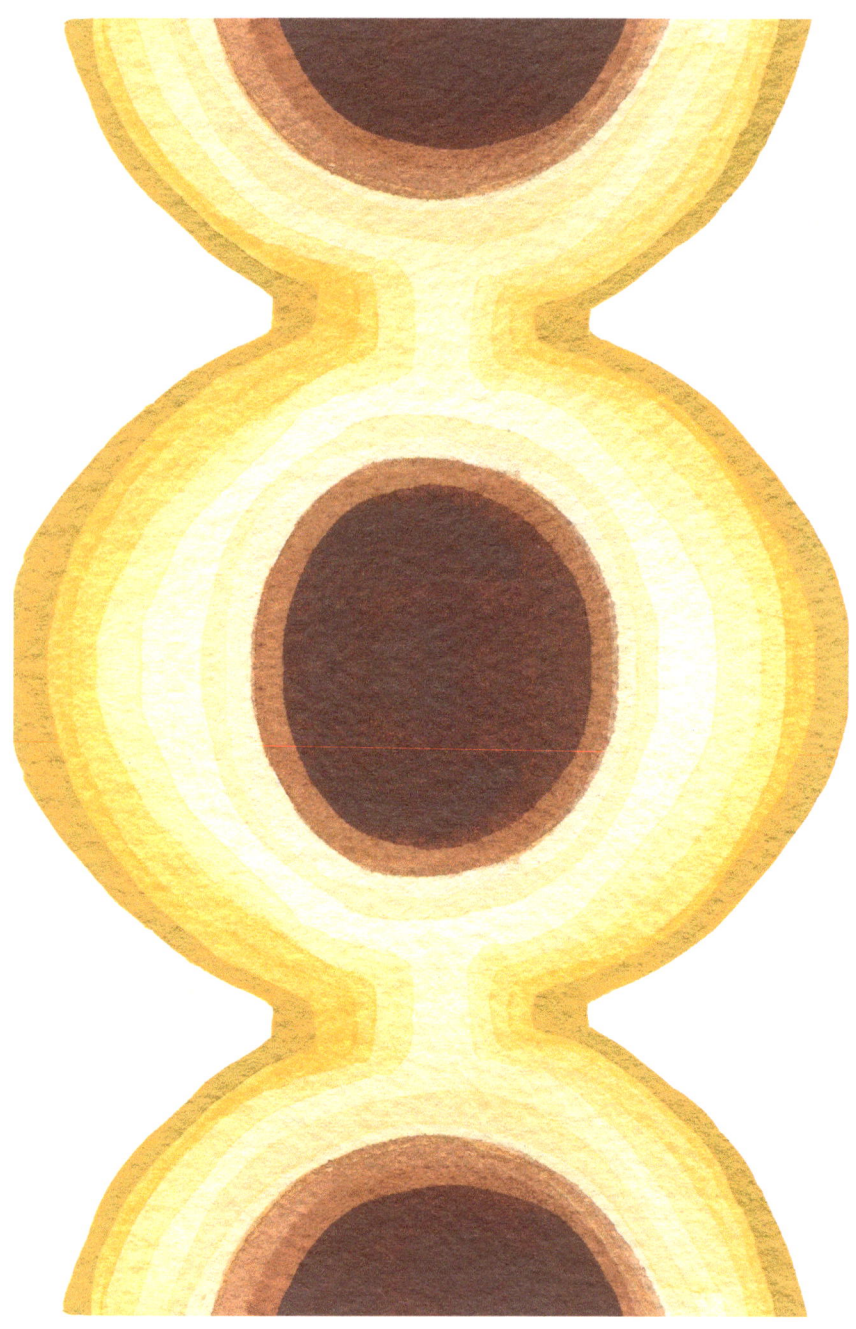

LESSON:
Interconnection. I am everything. Every action I make matters.

Punishment

"The festive lights in the city bring memories bittersweet,
The heart skips a beat again, the eyes yearn to meet.
Words alone are indescribable of what I feel,
why traverse that path again that will leave me
desolate and discrete?
Love unfortunately doesn't understand logic,
It's ready to prepare the soul for punishment,
in lieu of just one moment with you through a rare feat."

LESSON:
Pain brings me to growth and wholeness.

Justice

"O Lord, where did you find the glass to weave the fibers of my heart,
Why didn't you find the elastic with which you built theirs?
Mine was shattered into pieces so quickly,
theirs bounced back without needing any repairs.
You know I was in the deepest of love,
were they just afraid or callous or mistrusting?
I'd like to think they were Bezaire.
I deserve to know the truths, I'm not unreasonable,
O Lord, in your courts of justice & righteousness, just be fair."

LESSON:
Everything happens in its own time, with its own rhythm.

Traces

"I changed places, I changed faces,
I wandered the globe, I couldn't change my soul,
there's no one else it embraces.
I got busy, I pretended that I'm happy,
I know it's important to smile as it hides the tears it displaces,
When will my corpse release the soul it encases?
I'll wait for that day for it to fly to be where it ought to be,
it will even suffice with their traces."

LESSON:
I can reach inside myself to meet my own needs here and now.

Ponder

"I ponder with profound poignancy,
Despite incessant effort, why is there a constant deficiency?
The soul wanders in punishment, what was the delinquency?
Why did He choose me to go through this pain, what is His contingency?
I just need peace and rest, will it require an action in exigency?
Why aren't my prayers getting heard, why such stringency?
O Lord, relieve me or retire me, I'm tired of exhibiting resiliency."

LESSON:
Be steady and patient. Share needs, speak feelings honestly and courageously.

Mistake

"We talked, we walked, we shared a common plate,
We listened to the heartbeats,
I thought we had our story written on a common slate.
We held hands, we spent moments together,
I thought our emotions were sincere and oblate,
And then you just left, solitude was my fate.
It was so tough to realize that I was in love,
and you had made a mistake."

LESSON:

Self is complete.

Sparkplug

"The air is chilly, I yearn for the warmth of your hug,
I wish I could hold you in my arms snug.
The feeling of your breath close to mine, works like a psychedelic drug,
Your hair over my face, gives my heart a magnetic tug.
Why are you so far away, I want to feel your touch,
It ignites like a sparkplug."

LESSON:
I honor the different path I take from those I love.

Friendship

"We're not together, 'tis my destiny,
There's so much in common, why this complexity?
I was once someone special, now not even an entity?
Stubbornness with a purpose is perseverance, without it is entropy.
I know they're not inconsiderate, perhaps they fear our chemistry,
Is it that I'm breaking my own rule of 'no expectation,'
I don't want to be known for my elegies.
Mistakes have long being forgiven, friendship is at their clemency."

LESSON:
Let devotion be to truth, not object.

Worship

"Love is love, it is never wrong,
It is His choicest blessing; He picked my heart for it, 'tis His norm.
Love is ethereal, it does not need a physical form,
It is not an obsession, it's a devotional storm.
Seeing you or having you ain't a requisition,
I'll love you in each breath and action, like I love Him with aplomb."

LESSON:
How to breathe into the cycle of confusion and disorientation, and find a path forward..

Unknown

"'Unknown unknown,' I believed the magic was real,
How we found one another was surreal.
Dreams were woven and then dismantled,
Like burst fireworks, I dazzled at first and then became immaterial.
If all's done and dusted, why does the soul still feel queer,
'Tis the season of hope and healing, I pray for the holiday cheer."

LESSON:
Be here now. Be captivated by the present moment

Snowflakes

"The snowflakes invigorate the nostalgia of our togetherness,
The twilight reminisces of moments spent with one another.
The season has a new fondness,
for it brings memories of love in its splendor.
There isn't a single breath without your essence in it, 'tis an honest fervor.
Why didn't the time stall to let the flower blossom to its full color?
'Tis I'll ask Him at His altar after this life is over."

LESSON:
Intense emotions/feelings are normal, and it is not unreasonable to experience anger.

Conversations

"Long conversations were forgotten,
Emotions became irrelevant.
I was expeditiously disposed in the 'wrong' basket,
Without consideration or benevolence.
I was the 'most important person' once,
In the blink of an eye, my existence became irrelevant,
Change is the only constant, the lesson is now permanent.
It wasn't 'just an eye contact,'
the innermost feelings were bared transparent,
I was barely an attractive stop in a fast highway
that couldn't sustain resplendence."

LESSON:
When emotions are in opposition, no one is right or wrong. Both perspectives can be concurrently true.

The End

"'You're saying this to make me feel bad,'
was the response to my life-altering actions,
Befuddled I was with the comprehensions.
What else could I have done,
I was struggling for options.
Where did the kind person I trusted go was my only question,
I left it to Him and Karma to dispense
that I was sincere with my innocent emotions.
I'll wait for the day when I'm vindicated in His institution."

LESSON:
How to center into the self and welcome what is.

Zephyr

"The cold wind reminisces of moments we spent together,
Why did you go away, leaving me alone with storms to weather?
I crave to spend time with you, why does He not listen to my prayers altogether,
What did I do to be bestowed with this destiny, I have become untogether.
I am drowning in an eerie solitude, my spirit needs a propeller,
I yearn for your presence, my wings need a zephyr."

LESSON:
Some emotions only need to be felt.

I Miss You

"The glitter in your eyes, I miss you.
The shimmer in your smile, I miss you.
The warmth of your hands, I miss you.
The belongingness of your hug, I miss you.
Those long conversations, I miss you.
Those weekend expeditions, I miss you.
The silence of our togetherness, I miss you.
Only God and the moisture in my eyes know,
how much I really miss you."

LESSON:
Love exists without object. "I love" does not need a landing point.

True Love

"Trust was bestowed in what was said,
For not every word needs a promise.
Something went awry when 'It was all about you'
supplanted 'I miss our weekends.'
'A-teams' became blocked lists,
Even eyes shy to meet now.
Through this all, you flipped like a tossing coin,
but I stood steady like a rock, feet held strongly by love.
Love learns to forgive and let go,
I'll always give you the benefit of the doubt,
For I know you're a beautiful soul
who still needs to traverse this route.
True love is unconditional,
it is constant like the Sun and the Moon,
I'll always be there for you,
in drought, snow or monsoon."

LESSON:
Integrate the available lesson. Bring it back to the self
by taking responsibility. Don't blame another for your emotions.

Far Away

"I read in ancient transcendent texts, 'Love will find a way.'
Why did we cross seven seas to meet, only to go astray?
You're the witness to my love, O Lord, why're we so close, yet so far away?
Promise that you'll not do this to us again, in our next life in your play."

LESSON:
I respect that the journey you're on is different than my own.

Perfect

"'Perfect' is how they described us,
I was the 'complete package.'
And then like a one-time outfit,
I was put on and disposed in the forgotten closet.
'This is not what I want,'
those words were dispensed in a cold-blooded fashion,
I still shiver to see those eyes lack any remorse or emotion.
I put my neck on the line, perhaps I was naive,
I was an emotional fool who thought I was doing this for us to thrive.
Let bygones be bygones, I'm still in love for they're innocent at large,
I've always prayed for their fulfillment and success, I've never held any grudge in the heart."

LESSON:
Growth hurts, but in time truth is clear to see.

Swan Song

"This is my swan song.
Time has passed, life has moved on.
I know you're divine, God's own form.
I've the humility to bow down and say, 'You were right, I was wrong.'
I'll always love you, and pray for you for long.
May you find happiness and love in the place where you belong.
I hope we remain connected till it's time to leave for the heavenly town."

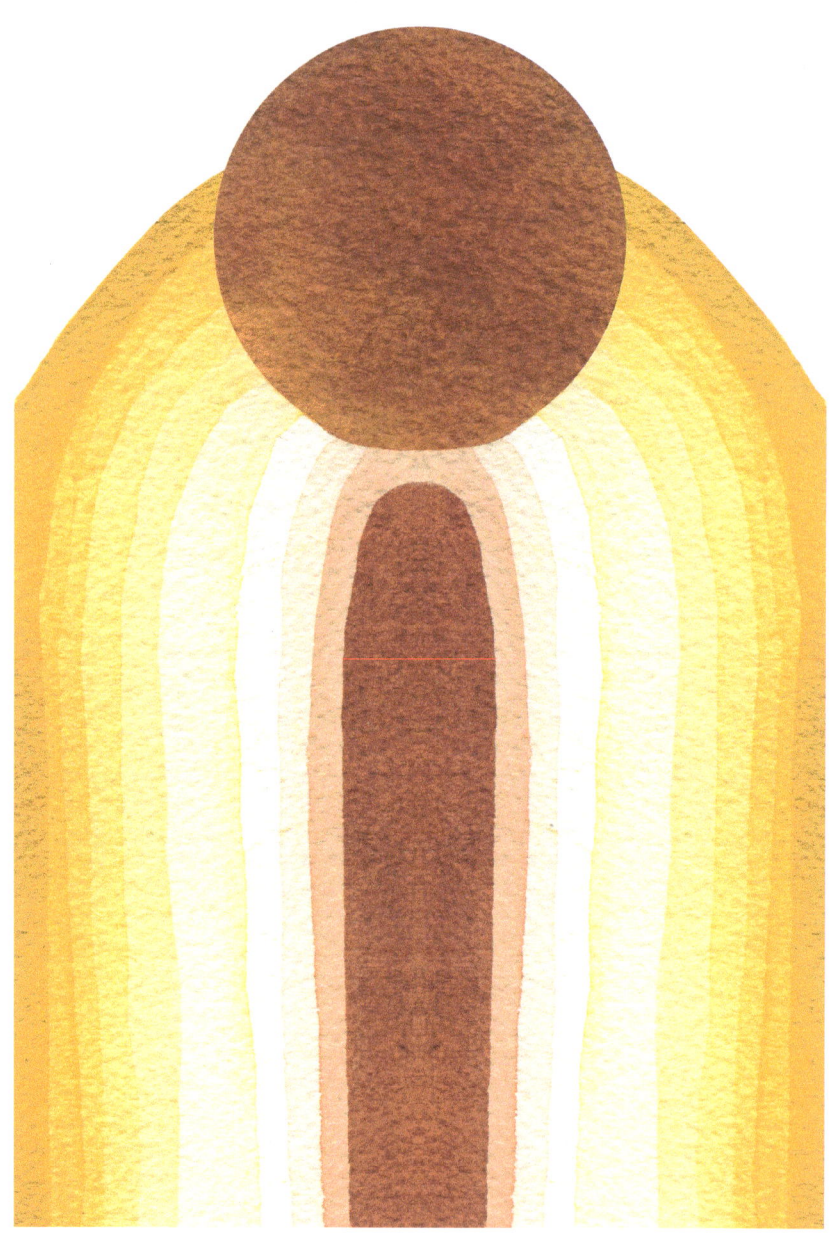

LESSON:
Trust that the pain will bring great truth and beauty in time.

One Day

"'One day,' they'd say to the vision I thought we shared in common,
I went all out chasing it, only to learn that I was operating in vain, solemn.
They changed, at first to do what's right,
Then they caught me off guard. 'That day will never come,' they said,
eliminating my existence as a blight.
I'd still thank them for gracing my life,
For it's because of them, I learned what it is to be selfless and in love, like
His own bright light."

LESSON:
Find your true need beneath the intense emotions.

Moments

"They live in the moment, I guess that's the way to live.
Some moments change lives forever, perhaps that thought remains elusive.
I was just another moment that passed,
I was an exotic experience that wasn't good enough to last.
Remember me for love, I will love you till the last breath.
I pray you find someone who loves you more than myself."

LESSON:
Even when I believe I'm unworthy, I'll rise into my fullest truth and love again.

Phoenix

"At first, they were enamored.
Then, like a receding high tide, they said,
'The attraction has faded away.'
The burn was akin to the touch of a burning coal,
It decimated the soul.
Now just the ashes remain,
With the glimmer of a hope of resurrection like the rare Phoenix."

LESSON:
Life will leave traces on us. What matters most is not that those imprints exist,
but rather that we integrate those lessons and choose the path of consciousness.

Footprints

"'Give this time,' I was told,
How much, I wasn't.
'You'll move on,' I was told,
How to, I wasn't.
They forged ahead as if I was just a misstep;
They didn't even look back to see how deep the footprints were.
I too created a perception of their erased footprints;
Little did they know that they were engraved deep within."

CPSIA information can be obtained
at www.ICGtesting.com
Printed in the USA
BVHW051333310521
608485BV00001B/2